WHAT THE DEAD WANT ME TO KNOW

Janet E. Aalfs

Also by Janet E. Aalfs

Full-length collections:

Reach, Perugia Press, 1999
Bird of a Thousand Eyes, Levellers Press, 2010

Chapbooks:

Against the Odds, Pennyroyal Press, 1981
Of Angels and Survivors, Two Herons Press, 1992
Full Open, Orogeny Press, 1996
Red, Thousand Hands Press, 2001
Lubec Tides, Thousand Hands Press, 2007

Many thanks to the small presses, generous editors,
and enthusiasm from all directions
that made these books possible.

WHAT THE DEAD WANT ME TO KNOW

Janet E. Aalfs

Published by Human Error Publishing
www.humanerrorpublishing.com
paul@humanerrorpublishing.com

Copyright © 2022
by
Human Error Publishing & Janet E. Aalfs
All Rights Reserved

ISBN: 978-1-948521-73-4

Cover artwork by Joann W. Aalfs,
hooked yarn tapestry, c. 1985.

Human Error Publishing asks that no part of this publication be reproduced or transmitted in any form or by any means electronic or mechanical, including photocopy, recording or information storage or retrieval system without permission in writing from Janet E. Aalfs and Human Error Publishing. The reasons for this are to help support the publisher and the artists.

With Love and Gratitude
Always

For Janis Ann Totty

For my family of origin –
Joann, John, Tom, Mark, Linden

For the Ancestors

ACKNOWLEDGMENTS

Poetry being both a solitary and collective endeavor, there are many who have contributed directly or indirectly to the making of this book, and who help to sustain its ongoing life, including you, dear reader.

Eternal thanks to Sally Bellerose, a phenomenal writer, storyteller, community activist, stellar human being, and cherished friend.

For enlightening conversations, gifts of friendship, creative adventures, and artistic inspiration, I am hugely grateful to James Arana, María Luisa Arroyo, Nobuntu Ingrid Askew, Anthony Chavez, Deb Curtis, Fatima Dike, Diana Ferrus, Marin Goldstein, Jillian Hanson, Beth Holt, Judith Katz, Kelly Keller, Reggie Marra, Amihan Matias, Marianela Medrano, Malika Ndlovu, Ed Sims, Jaye Spiro, Susan Stinson, Toni Stuart, Wen Mei Yu, Brian Zawilinski.

I appreciate my family of origin for offering me the world, and for their loving support on this poetic healing journey of life: Tom Aalfs, Mark Aalfs, the late Joann W. Aalfs (1923-2021), John L. Aalfs (1922-2001), Linden Aalfs Welch (1951-2020).

Ongoing gratitude to the people of Colcord, West Virginia – Homeschool, Sycamore, the Little Green Church – for being my original loving ground, for helping me to learn what true community means, and for working to save the mountains, including Barb and Gary Anderson, Etta Mae Cooper, Polly and Phil Pettry, and the late Okey and Thelma Pettry.

I am grateful always to teachers who are with me in spirit, including Leonie Amazeen, Gloria Anzaldúa, Lucille Clifton, June Jordan, Audre Lorde, Thomas Lux, Remy Amador Presas, Adrienne Rich.

And to Janis Ann Totty, my deepest love, admiration, and appreciation for daily encouragement, skillful suggestions, and brilliant artistry of all kinds.

Thank you to Paul Richmond of Human Error Publishing for his skill, generosity, and good humor in helping to bring this book to life.

My gratitude to the following publications in which these poems first appeared:

Contemporary American Voices, January 2013: The Meeting, Starcraft, Preacher; *VerseWrights*, March 2013: segments of 33 Lovesongs for Coal River Mountain; *Silkworm #7*, Spring 2014: The Question, Sunlit (Honeybee); *No, Achilles*, Waterwood Press, 2015: Sonnet for the Stolen Girls; *30 Poems in November! 2016*, Levellers Press, 2017: Shadow's Cloth (Bright Rose [and shadow]); *Celebrating Writers of the Pioneer Valley, 2017 Anthology*, Gallery of Readers Press: Heron Mystic Artist, Ascension, A Bird's Tale, A Simple Word; *VerseWrights,* 2014-2017: Metaphysics of Doubt, Original Nassoon (My Father's Voice), A Bird's Tale, Anne Jeanette's Tapestry, Ascension; *Nasty Women Poets, An Unapologetic Anthology of Subversive Verse*, Lost Horse Press, 2017: Queer; *Compass Roads*, Straw Dog Writers Guild, Levellers Press, 2018: Small Notes of Light, Swallowtail at Paradise Pond; *Silkworm #11*, 2018: Unlikely Bloom; *Silkworm #12*, 2019: At Some Point; *Silkworm #13*, 2020: Icicles; *Many Hands*, Fall 2020: Like Listening Underwater; *30 Poems in November! 2019*, Levellers Press, 2020: Not One But Thousands; *Hey, I'm Alive,* Spring 2020: Imagine She, Ars Poetica: Bird Cage, Su Hui's Star Guage, Duet.

CONTENTS

Prelude
Song for My Heart

I. PICTURE OF THE TURNING SPHERE

A Single Music   3
Icicles   5
Eternal, She   6
Queer   7
Forsythia   8
Upside-down in a Storm   9
Ars Poetica: Bird Cage   10
O : : Pen   11
At Some Point   12
Amaryllis   14
No Other Dance   16
Water Moon Guanyin   17
Channeled Whelk   18
Like Listening Underwater   19
Broke   20
Unlikely Bloom   21
Small Notes of Light   22
The Meeting   24
Sunlit   25
A Spark Within   26
The Question   27
Cuneiform   29
Mount Sumeru's Echo   30
Duet   31
Original Unfolding   32
Threads   33
Strangers   34

II. 33 LOVE SONGS FOR COAL RIVER MOUNTAIN

Away Returning: #1-11   39
Road: #12-22   47
Grit: #23-33   56

III. WE FOLLOW WINGS

A Bird's Tale   67
Ascension   68
Chicken Soup in Tepoztlán, 1976   69
Swallowtail at Paradise Pond   70
Brú Na Bóinne   71
Giraffe's Music   72
Anne Jeanette's Tapestry   73
My Father's Voice   74
Reflected Wings   75
Starcraft   76
Folded Shadow   77
Jonathan's Cloak   78
Julius's Shoes   79
The Journey Now Requiring   80
Shadow Cloth   81
Sonnet for the Stolen Girls   82
Imagine, She   83
Calm   84
Monwabisi's Sankofa Scarf   85
Traversing Chasms   86
A Crown of Sonnets for Mercy   87
A Simple Word   91
Metaphysics of Doubt   92
Not One But Thousands   93
Before the Word   94
Lightning   95
Heron, Mystic, Artist   96

Notes
Review
About the Author

Before our body existed
One energy was already there.

Sun Bu'er, 12th century China

Prelude
SONG FOR MY HEART

slower than thought
you have grown
quieter more watchful

leaf prints on the sidewalk
whispers brushing the wall

there go your poems before me
there goes your voice

your freedom the branches sing of
your insurmountable grief

blood-bright gifts
staining the ground
one-two one-two breathe step

oh how I live
for a single trace of your meaning
there goes the wind

all I have found
that is worth this world
you gave me

I
PICTURE OF THE TURNING SPHERE

A SINGLE MUSIC

1. Su Hui's Star Gauge

Moon on water following
      a single music
        radiant beauty for no one

stitched the temple pond
      so much gone
      so far away

Su Hui rhymed and spun
like stars embroider the sky
      petals of light disheveled

in one spiraling thread she wrote
clouds on silk that overlap
      mysterious appearance achieved

thousands of lyrics forward back
her xin unfurling here
      as tangled glories flourish

in ever-changing wind
words from nothing begin

2. Yu Wen Mei's Taiji

In opera's thin disguise
she sang to the jade woman
        luminous face adorned

who worked the shuttles before her
dark and light as plum
        in empty rooms

government banned
her taiji wings resilient
        I think only of the way

she strode across
bamboo bridges over lotus
        shared song can resound

all the way to this
in a courtyard in Suzhou
        as tangled glories flourish

an ancient wisteria vine
climbed its own shadow into sun
        a single music

roots deeper than doubt
Star Gauge drew me in
        radiant beauty for no one

like a gong's concentric pulse
shimmering gold and rose
        that does not end

ICICLES

For being continuous, there's nothing
like water. I wouldn't have known
how else to explain
the music in my mother's hands.

These days though she can't remember
words like pocket and snowshoe,
notes from her fingertips drip
as if there's a river under the snow

where one song meets
every song, and she's not afraid
to go there. Into the gully
behind the house, icicles fell

from the eave they lined like Yeti's teeth.
Trees on the hillside, shadows' flat blue
humming touched that glare.
If one broke off and you were standing there

it could knock you out.
For being memorable, there's nothing like
what never happened.
I watched my father watch

each fiery drop
hit the ground in silence.
That's how I knew
I could disappear.

For not looking away
I was given this prize.

ETERNAL, SHE

Body pressed to aquarium glass, chasms,
whorls, dark holes, so miniscule

my sea sponge lungs, you'd think she couldn't feel
the girl I was, breast buds sparking

hunger-pulse alive. Magnetic waves within
liquified my spine

coral
       baleen
              carapace
                      shrine

She opened her mouth
wider than doubt

breathing me into her spell.
Through brine-stung eyes I fell

into the eye
of every silence.

QUEER

When my mother at the table noted
the roast tasted queer,
I watched my father stare
as if to freeze the air
that sizzled like spit
on an iron skillet
      and disappeared.
No one saw me
      gone.
Every nerve and current burned
      my wordless tongue.
Like the slap he had meant
to stop a boy
from kissing me, or worse,
the girl he did not see, silent
lips to mine.
I trusted every feeling.
      My ground.
      My spine.
And learned the meaning
of mercy then – love
blessed that word my choking
parents swallowed to live.
      And pierced my heart.
      And pushed me out.

FORSYTHIA

yellow blooms reflected sun
                      true as a brand
like a sword my mother gripped
                      new leaf I twirled
  that bulk of stems two-handed
                      silence
      flared in the light
                      lemon amber gold
  devotion flooding our bones
                      sparks through the rain
      she painted
                      stroke by lucent stroke
    a plein-air portrait
                      palette brazen
      showing me how
                      my art could be
      through the fire
                      its every tongue
  what my father and she
                      spirals of smoke
    wrote on the wind
                      from a metal drum
  embers hissing skyward
                      her coils of canvas gesso oil
    these flowers I breathe

UPSIDE-DOWN IN A STORM

I hung by my knees
body of tree

roots and limbs
crows on the wind

no one there
but a girl drawn by the sound

bone-pulse down and down
lightning silent

blared through the leaves
thunder struck

pelvis to skull
clouds fell

and shadows of wings
into the creek whose witness carried

music of lost names to the sea
I studied my descendance

sudden rain drumming the ground

ARS POETICA: BIRD CAGE
after Chase Twichell and Irina Ratushinskaya

Like building a bird cage
out of birds

I tie words together in lines
and expect them to sing.

Like being a child.
Like being a cloud.

Something I can't imagine
any other way.

Like a hand grenade, a hand-
made poem.

Like nothing
I already know. Woman

to woman, tongue to lips, words
on a matchstick

slipped through a crack
in the prison wall ignite

an explosion of ink-
black wings.

O :: PEN

                        O   and O again
                    pen   O
        in the breathing   pen
                  light   in the breathing
                  first   light
             owl alone   repeats
          wing to wing   spiraled line
         a palindrome   ripples glisten
     sharp as a quill   stitch the water's skin
    writing the world   stars and rain
       of humming   nectar sings
bird hungry for red   tongue of gold
             lipped trumpet
     tongue of gold   bird hungry for red
       nectar sings   of humming
        stars and rain   writing the world
stitch the water's skin   sharp as a quill
      ripples glisten   a palindrome
       spiraled line   wing to wing
           repeats   owl alone
              light   first
    in the breathing   light
                pen   in the breathing
                    O   pen
      and O again   O

AT SOME POINT

Everything comes to a point – pine
bough and crown – at some point,
my mother chimes, memory a crystal

ball, cracks glinting, thicker clouds.
Snowbank, finger, depth and slant, shadowed
corners we see

how the world repeats
point by wandering point
above and below. Assembled as if

this moment to view
in snowmelt I push
her wheelchair through –

window, icicle, chimney –
reflected she glides
laughing to land

buried in glitter, snowflake skin
blood has heated to an apple glow.
I hand her a snowball

to throw – perspective
without any point – beyond
the field in which it will fall. Beautiful

arc. We follow the sun
across the frozen expanse
toward Angel Mountain. Frost

of breath, owl's gold eyes, blue
spruce, then sky. At the peak
the way becomes

slow, then slower until
we are nowhere
we have been before

like someone curled
beneath an avalanche
dreaming of lilacs.

AMARYLLIS

More delicate but more enduring
than a monument in stone.
        Ca Dao Vietnam

Like someone praying
in a prison cell, I imagine

my mother blooming, young
as a flower, though green

cannot find her, spine bent
as regret must bend

not giving in
but shifting, like the pale

yellow stem, how it managed to grow
at all in a box she would have praised

such gumption: leaf-spear stunted,
bulb shrivelled, petals

though crumpled flaring
like a broken promise

dreams of light repair.
How her garden flourished.

Peonies bold as drumbeats.
Lilacs, laughter, ferns.

Patterns she made from nothing
she knew before

their colors found her
ready to know

the way we would unfurl
as waves from the deep.

I in her, she in me,
edges spinning gold to green,

words we didn't really need, dancing
forever lit by the wild uncharted sea.

NO OTHER DANCE

I hold my mother's face
a map of lines
my palms imprinted trace
I stroke her limbs
no other dance
more perfect than
our wings aligned
expanding
dark mouth wide
last breath in
the curtain breathed her
flying out
through branches into stars

I cradle her
unwritten face
smoother than a stone
ocean-tumbled orb of moon-
lit granite in my hands
her gift this
tideswirl spine to spine
dervish spell
she has pulled me in
simple as a stone to find
anywhere you go
she reaches down
to show me

WATER MOON GUANYIN

*She who pays heed to the sounds –
and the cries – of the world*

Note by note, soft as a coral bell, she broke through glass.
Clouds and footsteps echoed. I followed as if in a dream

I awoke further into the dream to a garden alive
beyond walls between us we never meant to obey.

Though it hurt to walk on marble gravel, hand in hand
a familiar arc, I did not falter until

she gazed at me. Imploring. Wordless, I agreed.
We left the singing path. Cherry petals floated

into our hair unnoticed. Crimson tulips curled
inward as they burned. Lighter than a leaf

sacrum pelvis knee, moon-drawn, I turned to find
she had already strode clear through me.

CHANNELED WHELK

Within the spine
    another spine, memory
        a ribbon of eggs. Venus necklace

strung in silence. Countless
    perfect specks become
        large pear-shaped bodies

of turreted whorls.
    Buffy blue-gray sculpture,
        such fine revolving lines,

within memory, another spine
    small as a grain of sand begins
        the wordless form that ends

hurled from surf to shore.
    Empty then, held to an ear
        like a mirror the ocean sings.

Wind, heartbeat, tidal
    pulse, base to crown
        at the suture, a broad and deep

channel spells a winding
    terrace of dreams. Twisted columellas
        cut into elongate beads: onikó:lha'

each tongue-touched curve,
    each mother-word forgotten here
        yet lost, yet found.

LIKE LISTENING UNDERWATER

Something begun in shadow
rises from below the bridge

black river to silver sky
a heron light as mist

distant   yet here
like every moment layered

like listening underwater
stones clapping sharp as grief

wound to scar
softer stronger

brusquely dense yet feathered
I can hear my voice

tremble and bend
like the orchid stem

in a pink pot by the window
heavy with blooms

petals lit by crimson veins
shiver in the tattered air

then false words dissolve
and slide down our faces

in the silence of this
forever   love

I can taste
the salt we're made of

BROKE

I broke the stone
I broke

I did not mean
to fracture

the speckled stone
dark and light as moon

I clapped between
my two soft palms

like cymbals full of sun
two granite stones

one cracked
the other whole

I kept on dancing lifted
as ocean wave

and rock-strewn shore
together make a song

beyond the breaking

UNLIKELY BLOOM

I shone a flashlight down
the morning glory's throat
open in the autumn dusk

as I had never seen.
Though other blooms twisted tight as spindles
this one dared

a single flare
of longing into night,
tenacious word:

Hope.
A sound no image holds
spun within.

As cold air met
blood-warm breath
the purple funnel shivered.

I saw the horn
of a gramophone that
before it was made

did not exist.
Who could have ever
imagined it

unless she had heard
in the ink dark mist
a morning glory sing.

SMALL NOTES OF LIGHT

Leaves float on water, small notes
of light. The Mill River's slow
drift I wouldn't have noticed but
for this: you show me
moments in the world.

We sit on a rose-flecked
granite bench, Hospital Hill, sacred
Nonotuck ground, the lost
yet not forgotten
buried here unmarked

in a field we do not cross
to feel their shadows below.
You know what it is
to search, long and deep
for a cornerstone, dark cleft

in your hand, from all that was left
of your Nana's sod roof home
by the Celtic Sea. Who
of us will be the next
to go, and who to stay?

We are all carried away
by what we do
not know. Kinsale heath in her eyes,
she would have pointed to the hawk
spiraling over these graves.

She would have said, "I thought I told you
last time not to stare."
North Reading, kitchen dusk, lipton
steaming, all of us there, ceramic Santa
on the table, spinning around

and slower around until he faced
her rebel smirk, and the music stopped.
That's how we got
to laughing. That's how she made it
clear. Each memory

held by the next, edge
to edge, love's unfailing stitch
like glittering specks of mist
strung in a spider's web
on the gray steel bridge.

THE MEETING

Eyes on the ground, branches
bare, drawn like a flame-
blue thread through silken
mesh to the other side, I felt
my mind pulled upward, gaze
precisely tuned, no startle,
no flight, as dark antlers held
the light between us taut.
So skillfully the weaver stitched
our meeting fully shimmered.
That moment spread like wind
in feathers across the Oxbow.
Then a car appeared and a man
jumped out, phone in hand
to shoot. But all he got
were the trees the buck
had stood among more still
than my shadow, palms together,
fingers soft on lips,
and the sky kept bleeding
gold, and hoofprints in the leaves
told nothing.

SUNLIT

Imagine, how can you,
a drop of sunlit honey
falling from a spoon.
Such a sweet
language it speaks

from the world within
a hive, hexagonal rooms
warm as your tongue
holding the truth
of a thousand bees.

Imagine now, eternity,
a drop of sunlit honey
your hungry heart sings of
as the world swings
like a pocket watch

from your careful human hand;
and you love this
time we have
to imagine
however we can

that honeybees
and petals of light, blooms
from which we are fed
continue to unfold
amber, sapphire, gold.

A SPARK WITHIN

A spark within shifts the ground
to move me. I move
in points and curves. Everything swirls.
Even a murder of crows

the fog blows in from nowhere.
Listening, I become
softer, more clear, like an infant
before it can smile. I notice morning

sun breaks through. Past and future
branches weave. Even the wind
needs someone to touch.

Shivering web of air and rain washes me
awake. Apple blossoms flare, and a rabbit
nibbles spears so green its ears quiver fire.

THE QUESTION

It begins as an absence. In the dark
movie theater she appears

not to exist. On screen neither flying
kicks nor spins of her wit can be seen.

A good story, he said. But who would believe
a Buddhist nun developed the

system our hero delivers reel-
to-reel, bare chest rippling, iron grip.

Do you know the difference, I ask
in that high school library, between movies and real

life? A boy in the back shouts the challenge,
Could you fight Bruce Lee and win?

I'm standing before the artist as I answer,
We'd figure out how not to begin.

In words and gestures, forms flow; I honor
White Crane, legend and true. Ng Mui. Who

can prove her bones have not
led to these bones, sharp and soft

as columbine through cracks in rock? A girl
later in the hour, black hair draped over one eye, barely

raises her hand. Could you fight Bruce Lee and win?
I almost ask did she hear me before, about

to repeat myself, when I realize what
her question is not. I can see in her other eye, light

falling from a thousand wings,
she wants me to promise I'll survive.

CUNEIFORM

How can you be
      any good   meaning
already clear   when you learn these
      arts from women
quantum dust   salt rose   deer
her stylus speaks   etched in bone
      kunta quna queer
cuneiform of blood
      how dare you
      be
      so here
written wild   not good not bad
      how a grain of sand
incites a pearl   irritation's gift
      moon in the dark
sky of shell   more luminous
      than any word
      unknown until
      she opens

MOUNT SUMERU'S ECHO

Far from Mount Sumeru
my worn-out horse threw me.

Nothing left to grip
the iron bell struck bone. Falling

from the ground I rose
lighter than wind.

Thousands of miles and lives beyond
lightning spears the summit

as hooves thunder within
her silent echo.

DUET

    to spell the duel : : duet
        nipa leaves resound   her absent name
  through drought and rain   these sinawali rhythms
          ta   ta   ta-tung   through smoke and flame
        no hand can quell   tata-tung   tung   tung
              Alin Ed Purowa
          her até spirit's weave
            rattan stalks ignite
           constellations within
tata-tung   tung   tung   no hand can quell
through smoke and flame   ta   ta   ta-tung
  these sinawali rhythms   through drought and rain
      her absent name   nipa leaves resound
            to spell the duel : : duet

ORIGINAL UNFOLDING

Though I don't recall
the exact dance, it lives

in my cells. I see us
in a wide expanse

beginning
each in an egg,

breaking through
cracks of shell

our feathers at first
wet in the light.

Then a fluttering
wind draws us up

to stepping, kicking, spinning.
And we turn

into ourselves, becoming
each other's mirror.

Leaf, hand, branching
veins, grace unfolds

in the scent of green
grass on our skin, sun

in our breath, sweetfern
by the river.

THREADS

I watched her open
a spiral of hair
the way I remember
dividing embroidery thread
one strand into many
each able to slip then
through the eye
of my needle multiplying
the number of stitches
I could sew

Now I recognize
that long ago
motion in her hands
able to find
in every breath
the listening
uncoils a fiber
the weight of light
between us
stars that guide
and blossoms to mark
the crossroads
stitching
freedom's quilt

STRANGERS

I am a stranger
learning to worship the strangers
around me.
         June Jordan

1.

an ostrich egg traveling to Mars
who can fathom

the white body
detached from its own construction

how cruel inside forgetting it grows
who can imagine

here in our hands
the broken shell   *we must*

the woven space   *imagine*
rounder softer darkly flaring

within and beyond
it's all music

interstices and patterned lines
call us to cultivation

who doesn't want to dance
learning to notice

the look on your face already amazed
to admit the jasmine

2.

gasoline fumes and dry leaves swirled
as the tinted glass hummed downward

I leaned my face that close to his
our bodies crossing black and white

lines we breathed
in the tangled dark

easy here he smiled
to lose your way

chill wind blew through my sleeves
in the silence between

a poem can turn
anywhere

he named the steps and I repeated
three four five times

left right left right burger king that's it
write it down

and I did
and he almost let me go

geese skeined through the city night
I could hear their wings

but he was not able
to stand the thought of me

lost somewhere

so he drove slowly through the maze
to the parkway entrance

and I flashed my highbeams
in the wake of grace

3.

who doesn't want to dance
within and beyond

like cranes soaring through thunder
shifting now on the wind

how much can be done with how little
face that close to a stranger's face

learning to hear you
I become myself all over again

in the music finding
not what we die for

all this to live

II

33 LOVE SONGS
FOR COAL RIVER MOUNTAIN

AWAY RETURNING

In my chest wings beat harder
In my blood rivers then stones

1. 1960 : : 2010

        Mountains still
                redbird trills
     close as mourners
                complex cells
   grave too fresh to kneel
                 roots unfurling spell
   train rocking   north
                  the ground
        star bright away
away   I wanted to touch
          green curves
      but the glass shone
           too cold

    Steady in the sway
                leaf to cliff
    a woman smiled
                in rapture
  from the seat behind
  her wrinkles spread like
wind on the river   clouds
                mountain high
    forever floating by
               notes clear
and the backs of houses
      broken down
and the sweet singing stream
  shimmered a tune I knew
              Coal River's aria
  of dulcimers and spoons

2. Hologram

Catamount and mountaingirl
hunger staring   eye to eye
names on the wind   butterflies
lemon mint unfurls   sun and sky
tawny fur   towhead's double
crown ignites   summit shrapnel
glints within   decimated shadows
     louder drills the silence
     colder drills the fire
     lupine and crickets cease
     nothing but coal dust speaks
catastrophic cinders
salting every meal
     bodiless
     a star shocks
     the distance
     light travels
     persistent
     and serene

3. Wishing

Bear went over the mountain to see
another mountain she could see
summits blasted into empty blue
the boy who shot her
roaming high up Sycamore Holler
wishing he could bring her back
didn't know she was the one
paw twisted limp
used to sit beside the garden
hyacinth and mint
a place she didn't have
to leave

Indigo and white
violets wake up

    I do
    not speak
    in long
    lines my feet
    remember miles of no
    words the way
    I place each quiet
    step to sunlit
    matter
    here I find what is
    the ground breathing
    paw to stone
    as dreams through skulls
    the wind scours
    bear
          me
                home

4. Scent

Forget the leaf
forget the vein
forget the spark
alive in seng
forget the river's
jewels of ice   laughing
stars and monarchs
flashing fiery wings
forget the summit blasted
forget the chestnut scent
the burning
roots I can't
forget

5. Cadence

In the undergrowth
a wren's intricate
warbling roots absorb
cadence of honey
syntax of milk brilliant
phrase in silken corn
rabbit the brambles hide
mountain language soft
spotted newt and
molly moocher's cap
protection fierce
the ribald nettle stings

6. Preacher

He opened the ground like a book
to plant his chosen words
in glistening soil by the headstone
that tilted like a body wanting
to fall into moon-drifts
    our long starving hopes
fearing the dark too close
in their eyes he shivered
like a golden bird
caged in the damp shaft
poison gas prayers dispersed
lighter than breath
    thine image
doubting his own music
he applied his hand
like a bandage
or a wound
    stamped upon this clay
irises that wilted
shoulders hunched in the chill

raindrops sliding through the gully
at the base of his feathered skull

7. Revelations

Dingy cast-iron stove slouched
at the center of a bare one-
room schoolhouse
flames swallowed logs
smoke snuck
through cracks to touch
Coal River Mountain
ridges stitched in frost
    a woman robed with sun
bone to bench stuck in ice
head bowed over letters
I learned to read the moral
snide rebuke to rule
of thumb rod unspared
the master struck
to mine the hills
and valleys of her
ancient haze smoke-blue
    beneath her feet the moon
scuffed shoes
on spark-singed floorboards
singing root to crown
I vowed to write
a book of revelations
as full of light
as any heart

8. Groundless

Stronger than fear   air-
borne dreams   rope across
the creek   swinging bridge
in the wind   stones
glistened   water-
skin   You couldn't help
but be   clouds blowing
through blighted trees   branches open
to the last page   distant
light rushed in   blasted
from the strip-   mine
pearl-white birds   shattered up
You lifted   every word
every leaf   You took
and left   in my hands
this empty
book

9. Ground

I look up to find
birds   nothing
but birds
in my chest wings beat harder
in my blood rivers then stones
spine a budding bruise
bonesongs fly from the mines
to show my body becomes the wind
nothing   but stones the wind
has carried here
to love

10. Cradle

Fifty years beyond
>*hush little baby*
>*don't say a word*

pulsing lullabies
faces recognized
>*as soon as you*
>*walked in I knew*

less than a speck
of time passed
>*exactly who you were*

in the Milky
Way she sang
a ladle full
of stars through
all those windows
by heart   certain
as the moon
rocks in a cradle
of hills we met
>*after the wedding*
>*Jimmy slipped your dad*
>*some money for marrying us*

Etta Mae won't waste
a single word
in the telling
>*your dad turned to me*
>*here he said you need it*
>*more than I do*

she opens her hand to show me
frayed and mended lines etched deep
now that neither Jimmy nor my father
live but here memory flares
as light through a prism separates
yet never
>breaks

11. Skin

Slopes close as skin
tongue to palm like a salt lick   black-
berries we picked near the rails   coal
train gone   whistle gone   mountain
top destroyed   nothing to hold
tree or cloud   swinging bridge
my mother gripped each kid
to cross   the flood ripped out
I have traveled far to taste this dark
blood a river cool and heavy
stones I never left within

ROAD

Here is your road, tying
you to its meanings: gorge, boulder, precipice.
Muriel Rukeyser

12. Pax

Don't go to Pax my friend
don't drive that unpaved
mountain pass
don't fork on Toney's Road
don't dare the steep
and narrow once
begun you can't
go back
no rail to stop you
flying down
the cliffs are grand
but you can't see
a thing for gripping
hard the wheel
don't follow clueless
maps he laughs
next time don't
go to Pax

13. Colcord

Peach Tree   Clear Fork
Spruce Mountain Road
so many hopeful words
for the singular way
that follows the creek
and lets me reach
     right here

used to be you had to criss-
cross riffles splashing hooves
stones and mud   wagon wheels
then coal rails Co Route 1
no map defines the heart
of Homeschool Village
Colcord West Virginia
gems you'll never find
from the highway yonder
driving toward vacation's
planned for destination
anywhere but here

14. Twin Angels

In the woods up Kayford Mountain
in a graveyard in the sun
I can feel my mother humming
redbuds blooming above
here twin angels kneel in the dirt
paper-whites and porcelain wings
such tiny things to keep the dead
from standing up to find
they hold the mountain steady
tooth to jaw to twisted spine
gaping in the dark
they watch the river swell
discolored scarf unraveled fishing
lines entangled the rowboat leaks
nothing left to do but
        speak
shiver they say
you better run
river rising
dark night fall
too cold they point
don't try to cross

bees is gone
spinning gold
light in the holler's
mouth drown
this bag we rattle
ribs and jags
our cloth float
not at all

15. *Post*

Condolence cards
tacked alive to the post
office bulletin board
everyone knows
someone who   why run
to escape the blues
no fast enough to leave behind true
music   returnreturn
letters shaped like cranes
unfolding paper
crease of wing
make music dance within
the word make
deeper word

16. *Montcoal*

Twenty-nine strands of light
the monument becomes
names gouged in stone
a place together to know
the way they were
at the last
not hoping
so much as

letting go
of the chance
to ever feel
lips again on their lips
breath on skin
becoming lighter than
or so it went
kissed beyond
as tenderly
a whisper kisses the night
each letter
of each remembered
name we call
a constellation
any love
can touch

17. Well

Bright as blood embroidered threads
erupt from roots of laurel blooming
Kentucky legend on horseback
Red River his Cherokee
maw-maw carried constellations
leaving in her wake precise
stars in stamen petal leaf
sassafras and snakeweed
vein and fracture heal

Fiery green sun through trees
Okey's memory long as late-day shadows
Kayford Mountain throws
across close-knit yards
      there he says can you see
no icebox then
I'd lower the bucket
of cheese and butter

to touch the deep
chill below
    words he does not say
    you're free
    to draw from the spring
    to slake your thirst
    like rain on dust
my mother's water
broke beside that well
and I fell in
suspended
on a rope of light
from her to me

Same igneous edge to edge
arranged in every bone
since childhood known
in shadow games   hide-and-seek
hoping to be seen   they'd always found
the quiet underside of leaf
then softened steps through snow
watched each other grow
in balance beside the river
Thelma mixed the mortar
Okey hauled the stones
wrapped in pearl-gray wind
they built a true abode

In the front yard by the road
an orange Gulf sign tangled
in bittersweet still shines
though faded they refused to sell
even for a thousand dollars
a city slicker offered once
who could   not know the way
everyone used to go there
for petrol and pancakes
and something to say

18. Talking Matters

Stuffed and wrapped
free steamed dogs
slaw mustard ketchup
at the center talking matters
late for work hands flutter
wind water under-
stand he sends his daughter
money from the mine
tomorrow she'll drive to the capital
to speak for clean rivers
and jobs that don't destroy
the children   our only ground
meanwhile government rich old boys
launder money behind her back
fumbling hands in drawers
the same old way they did
in schoolyard shadows plotting
to take her out   she takes them on
do they think she doesn't know
heartbeat spilling blues
empty cupboards   no clean coal
spelled across   a brick wall mural
splintered now to factions
local grass-   roots trampled yards
chickens peck the dust
rib-thin dogs prowling streets
coal trucks wreck   she dares to see
(though boarded windows
make no shine)   past all that

19. Union Notes

Spine a quill
voices weave
tender lilt I
lost then found
difficult to hear
grace notes
her Blizzard grit
no thieving
mine track quells
veins of grief
mountain steep
refusing the choice
to kill or die
women tore up
iron rails
crowbar washboard harp
blood to ink 1912
halting deadly wheels
turned them clear
around to union
notes resounding still
silent cliffs keep watch
ceilidh of coal-
stained roots
chestnut redbud sycamore
echo bonelit melodies
creekborn holler strong
this blooming core

20. Motel

Her harley t-shirt glitters stardust
lemon-scented spray to swipe
she'll finish cleaning by noon
then cross the street to orchestrate
pants blankets jackets   necessary thrift
porcelain sunflowers emerald elves
need and whimsy stack the shelves
later silver wings unfettered
twisting mountain road through engine
roar and wind the sky her skin

Husband due at four
register and chiming door
white hair neat as a pin
he signs the miners in
to dynamite the summit
book in hand reading when he can
Oliver Twist he winks
then says his mother loved to think
he'd be a writer too

March wind hot   cup by cup
cooler almost drained
the owner warns him   stop it
but he looks the other way
as kids dash in to guzzle
then vanish into the waning light
split by diesel fumes they swallow
used to be they could drink the creek
now slurry turns it black
the moon floats belly up

In the best of times
and the worst of times
his name echoes notably   he is himself
a union man I'm very ooooold he grins
giving the O a victory spin

21. Collapse

Redbuds cling to cliffs
above the silent tracks
her fiddler frets
no longer hum
finger joints grow thick
giant trucks rumble coal
through narrow mountain passes
for floodlights on the highway
and screens that glow
bluish in the parlor all night long
company owned company named
Ameagle walls collapse
slag heaps spill   creeks gasp
fish float rotting down   music squeezed
can't sing the cancer out   its raptor screech
unchecked and we   don't learn
who dies for this

22. Tracks

Pressed to the page a pledge
her first poem bled
through fingertips in amber drops
and red stars on moss
no fairytale no ballad of love
she rose and You lay down
beside her vein to vein
too thin to hide   tracks dawn
lilacs sprung from her arms
buds the color of
mountains that cut
the sky from her voice

GRIT

The stones of the sanctuary
lie strewn at every street corner.
Lamentations 4

23. Temple

It's where the music
comes from I am
living as another
temple shattered   no one knows
how many more to go
(airline pilots steer
to avoid the ashen craters)
thrumming deeper   word on fire
it's where the music finds me
no blast can kill
her roots of ironweed
her redbird's trill

24. Ramps

Up Drew's Creek
women meet
every kind of wild
leek the long
table sings
to hear them
laughing April
wind sneaks in
through dogwood
stirring ramps
in fried potatoes
ramps in wilted
lettuce salad

ramps in eggs
cornpone grits
ramps relish
women mix
the tender raucous
taste of sun
piercing every tongue

25. *Rattlesnake*

Did you ever eat
rattlesnake
no but I had
iguana
did it taste
like chicken
we cackled
feathered and scaled
like biddies
by the fence
how do you fix it
in slices
it's difficult
to chew
are you scared
of getting bit
when you're hunting
and you hear
that dry hiss
like shale
slipping down
the hill

26. Post-blast

Lilac petals on windows
the blast
      shook
            loose
blossoms opened and fell
loud as hail on corrugation
      set upon by rage
and memory's coal-split eyes
fangs slice to the quick
no prayer stick shout
can interrupt   no story leaf
not even the wind   knees collapsed
blood congealed   is what you think
you're made of   spicy fragrance burns
path of knots and snags
brambled vines in the gorge
sting your face   steal your breath
jab by jab   multiplied
even the smallest   it
sounds like hit   pushing through
skin to blood to bruise
you did not choose

27. Shaft

Hidden within
blue-black scars
wave by wave
I swallowed until
the other shore
pushed me down
that wordless
shaft again
even silence
couldn't drown

salt
    star
        whalesong
silver chain
mama gave me kissed
my neck   iron chain
the coal boss hitched
between my legs tore
cloth and skin
I crawled through damp
to pick the seam
until I couldn't lift
that tool anymore
blessed or cursed
made no difference
I was a girl
I had no friends

28. Strides

Lightning scars
on birch bark
one hand jammed
in a pocket   thick
coal-stitched denim
pants designed
for men her body
strains against
the way she strides
through every seam and fiber
swallows taunt-laced air
never lost
her dreaming
pearl of black
sky on tongue
crow-black mouth
teeth of stone

blackberry pie
packed before dawn
lamp to lamp
third eye clear
as Venus
she dares
to drill the vein
tamp the clay
light the fuse

29. Got

Got my goat
got my hill
billy-clubbed our
Jack and Jill
tumbling down
Blair Mountain
rather wreck
than reckon
red bandanas blood
called redneck
    what's the use of all that
     noise and money   yonder
city's got to have it
lit so high got
coal got rich
cracked my fiddle
stole its tune
our own got
more determined
    converging gorges
     jumbled cliffs
these union horns
play sharper
notes than gold
through flesh to marrow

30. Cleft

He hands his mother
a sprig of quince
    rock of ages cleft
she wants to take
    they'd been singing
root in her yard
    in the little green church
the flood buried
    when the deluge struck
in sludge that filled
    from up the slope
every room and path
    giant tires had gouged
now blaring ATV's dig ruts
dust on the porch swing
wind's too hot   grit in her shoes
blood-stained axe by the door
he doesn't say what for
not the biggest snake
grown fat on mice
harmless as a whippoorwill
in the garden no moon
reaches tonight
but the copperhead
that could have struck
from its dark coil
on the shelf
can't find itself

31. Leaves

Rhythmic blade through shank
butcher block once
soaked in gristle
occupies a corner

beside the dining table
silent indentation
their father wore in wood
polished grain
her eyes contain
memory's layered ache
brother home for treatment
loved the fiery leaves
up Spruce Mountain
curving into sky
and down the other side
beyond the gold and crimson
of any living
voice they fly

32. Clocks

JB's got
time at least
a hundred clocks
no shelf chair
counter without
faces numbered
one to twelve
pluto tinker bell
snow white
pepsi coors aladdin
most need a battery
though the gold
pendulum swings
in the grandfather
clock his prize
the roof might
leak the window crack
nothing
keeps forever
laughing to be seen

JB's fine
as a frog's hair
he hollers across
the circular road
stones and sinkholes
sun high
waving at us
to stop

33. Heartstone

Barb spreads a quilt of roses
pillows plump as clouds
feather-stitched in sunsweet air
Gary fires the water tank
and checks the cellar for bears
barefoot girl he smiles
to feel that time in me
still running through the grass
this Appalachian lovesong
sun-filled manse of ladybugs
drawn through cracks
to window heat
fallen by the thousands
brilliant embers I sweep
from every sill and corner
as if those midnight
flames still burned
the upper house a pyre
as if my dreams could hold
wrapped in a blanket
wet from the creek
heartstone hidden
deep within
I never left

III

WE FOLLOW WINGS

Shadows in the fabric of birdsong.
Silence light as bones.
We follow wings
through the river asking
why have we feared death
as if it is not
also what sings?

A BIRD'S TALE

Many who die
become birds,
and dragonflies

in the marsh,
and rippling sun
on birch bark.

I'd like to be
one of these –
an original

Taiji sequence,
Grasp the Bird's Tail,
urges me to examine

its homonym, each
feathered word.
Later in the form,

more alive, Slant
Flying, I'm there.
Bones of lace

admit the sky. Moonlit
cliffs root us. Here within
You shimmer

and sing to us
as You glide: Love
is this, all

we will ever
need to know
about dying.

ASCENSION

I whispered.
Eyes closed.
I waited.
Neck still limp.
Beak darkly gaping,
the songbird's body grew
light as a shadow in my hands.
I had no face but the wind.
And though my prayer
enveloped me
I never thought
it would fly
huge and sudden
into the trees.
Between us
such daring.

CHICKEN SOUP IN TEPOZTLÁN, 1976

In clear broth gnarled
talons of a chicken curled

fierce and still
as if that bird hung

under the table, stubborn
foot stuck through

my bowl, and slept
and bound me

to dream, red
umbrella twirling

sparks marimba fires dance
on water Aztec lily morning

glory clenched unfolding
feathers of awe

SWALLOWTAIL AT PARADISE POND

On the evening shore a swallowtail
circles my body and drinks from the mud.

Ink-black spots and lines on yellow,
yellow on black, the fallen sun. A song has flown

from the dome of sky that ripples
in the bowl of pond. Indigo, Rengetsu's brush,

her hand revives wind in the reeds.
A butterfly, or a dream. On the hillside

hundreds of fairy irises bloom
and a flower called Inside-Out.

Hokke-kyo, I have learned the name
of a prayer for peace from a bird.

BRÚ NA BÓINNE
Newgrange, Ireland

At the tunnel's end
curled like a cat
in a granite bowl
in the darkest dark
before Stonehenge
before pyramids
in a mound of shale
and white quartz orbs
no gaps no need for mortar
she waited for the lizard
tongue of sun
to spark her song

not the point of why
not the cloudless sky
not the lottery I'd have to win
not the minutes
seventeen for winter
solstice to unroll

a path of gold
no thief could ever steal
nor guide explain
not the spiral forms she carved
listening deep within
as boulders quarried miles away
the ones who sang
sent floating down the river
a tower of clouds

not captured in a photograph
not burned in a Christian raid
not lost in time
this moment
her eye-light
the same as mine

GIRAFFE'S MUSIC

As the stone has been
misunderstood, and her wild
love maligned, and her still

bewildering music shunned,
so have I.
Lips soft as clouds, voice

so low you think me mute
as a shadow, I speak.
Loch Ness serpent's neck, gentle

tongue and teeth, leaves I eat
from the treetops sing their stories
inside me. Legs so high I stride

through lotus blooms and meteors.
I have listened longer than memory
to the heartbeat at the core of earth

and heard the stone of the quna,
cuneiform alive, as she wrote
the first human word.

ANNE JEANETTE'S TAPESTRY

Anne Jeanette sat down in the snowmelt,
shallow span of water she swirled,
quiet from the sky, painted
from the trees, her baby
brother, my father, asleep.
He drank those lullabies.
I watched through an upstairs doorway
hands conducting the wind,
a palindrome for balance.
And though she couldn't have heard me,
she offered toward my fingers
in response to the question unasked
a cat's cradle of words. Strings
at angles hummed and shifted,
gray from the rocks, sung
from the finches, rooted in asters,
purple and gold. Yes, this story, she said,
a pasque flower my father trampled
is the one I told to the hills,
seven miles there, seven miles back.
I was only a girl
walking the world
to be here.

MY FATHER'S VOICE

Perfidia at the station,
young men harmonize.
Train cars empty, lights

dim, an old man
humming in a wheelchair
could have been my father,

original Nassoon, singing
in the smoke of wartime
as the world kept swinging

on a rope of tunes
like one of those bath soaps
that smells like a lily, golden

strand at the center
woven through every cell,
a common note

you'll find if you listen closer
than a dream. Heart's refrain a spiral
stretched like a strand of pearls

reaching from earth
to the cobalt moon forever
in a glance, my father's voice

a gorgeous bloom among all
the voices lit
as the wheels of iron turn

back to the first
song we learn
in silence darker than blood.

REFLECTED WINGS

World War II courier bag
locked to his wrist,
onyx sky erupted orange
as lava, as thought,
enemy fighter's errant shot
too close to flee.
No oxygen mask,
no heated stone
to unfreeze his bones
in that soul-splitting hold.
Forget you were ever here,
my father swore.
I knew.
He never was
able to make it
stop. That other air-
craft plummeting
could have been
the one he crouched within
forever gone. Bodies,
stars, autumn leaves.
Cloud-white hair. Coma.
I know.
I was there.
I whispered blue fire words
in his ear. Falling. Not falling.
Herons camouflaged as rocks,
dozens stood in the Occoquan
as he took his last breath in.
Face drawn upward,
light in his wings,
he told me everything.

STARCRAFT

Stranded *Starcraft*, windshield jagged, sits
in a cornfield, tipped to leeward, hull full of leaves
and river sand from the Oxbow shore.
Winter wind must have floated
it in from Mars, no motor,
no gasoline, not even a ghost
to steer it through deeper currents
that hold me now. In the bow
a plastic rug, aqua as a swimming pool.
In the stern a purple ice tea can dented in rust.

My father loved salt mist on his arms
and sun splashing his face.
When I drove that boat
I was nothing less
than an osprey hitting the waves
eyes first, and the stun
of clear green ocean in my beak
shattered every sound.
All these years beyond
I'm only beginning to speak of
what I found.

FOLDED SHADOW

Tiles in the floor a labyrinth, we walked
the cavernous hall, and found our way
through echoing light to a simple chamber.

My father and I at the reading composed
side by side like stained-
glass windows, words

our bodies prismed until
we could not tell
whose listening shaped each ray

that danced and fled.
"That one," my father said,
"did you notice? He's depressed."

Poet whose folded shadow fit
like a tidal river within.
Scent of sulfur, mudflat glistening,

long ago at the shore, once
and only once, I asked him,
"Do you believe in ghosts?"

Something in the salt I breathed,
and my father's insistent doubting,
I could hear it, that song, treacherous

yet sweet, softly blooming
into the wind, the heart
of his words I wanted.

JONATHAN'S CLOAK

There's nothing thinner
than the skin of a man
who knows he'll die
too soon

still in love
with every man he loved
these bramble roses

sitting on a rock
in the garden beside
his mother's house

nothing so dark
as his eyes
surrounded by white
bones as he digs

lily-of-the-valley
spears in the shade
of lilac leaves

and nothing more
determined
than a fragile
wild bouquet

the van's whole roof
draped in a cloak of blooms
as he drives away

JULIUS'S SHOES

On Table Mountain
a tall man sang, Robben Island
in the haze beyond.
To the Lion my art-
blessed brother sang
in his bright red shoes.
I laughed, watch out
they'll fit me.

And just like that he left
footsteps big as craters
along the shoreline, striding yet
through townships, his rhythms glide
inciting every heart – *if you believe
in love, and you believe in miracles.*

Changing, he changed us, like dusk
stones we thought were seals
at the edge of breaking waves
pulled with graceful flippers
and vanished into the deep.

We watched that phantom ship approach,
black sails full of stars.
Gauging the tide he knew
his constellation had arrived,
not to carry him
far off, but this way
for all to cross.

THE JOURNEY NOW REQUIRING

The journey now requiring
countless arms as one
lifting
like a dogwood toward
the golden arc of sun
minus the flowers
minus the hands
holding bouquets
minus the
faces
we had no way
to gather
our mother close
to a century old
on the other
end of the line
silent
for a spell
her voice encrypted
like an iron bell
finally said to me
you're not dead yet
but now I see
days before it happened
she could hear
her other daughter
sinking underground
as the dogwood
in fierce and delicate tones
sang to be found

SHADOW CLOTH

Frayed white cloth she waves
perhaps a piece of curtain or
a shirt she wore
to school before
bomb-split doors
and pointed guns
footsteps in the dust
sharp debris and trucks
her mother grips the baby and
her little brother's hand
she walks alone behind
the fluttering scrap flies free
sun too bright to see
like a kite whose string
has snapped
or a brave balloon
calling her name
it could be noon
anywhere on earth
no lunch today
no jumprope
no echo of prayer
Oh   Ah   Om   Amen
wind through the lemon tree
she has climbed her shadow

SONNET FOR THE STOLEN GIRLS

The question a dark shirt, empty
sleeves grab her, dirt and cloth
in her mouth: What clothes were the men
wearing? What colors did they have on?

I feel afraid, she swallows, running
in the dark away. Silence slips between.
Were they uniforms? *I feel
afraid*, shivering, she speaks

from within the many dresses
pressed to the cold gray walls.
Their mothers wail: Where are they?

From the loaded truck she runs,
no question left, she flies. No answer
as the pants, the belts, the boots multiply.

IMAGINE, SHE

She, as you.
She, as I.

Even the one who stands behind
cheering him on.

All the leaves, every color
and shape, every size,

old ones, young ones,
sun-washed, rain-lashed,

turn in the wind.
We see them.

She as you as I,
light hidden on the undersides,

silver-soft, flutter and lift.
Even the one

who swears her man will save her.
Even she

remembers, tells it, weeps.
We hear them, so close,

wind in every wave.
Tides calm to raging

turn and turn and yet.
The one who smooths his brow

and kisses him to sleep.
Even she.

CALM

Last night I prayed
to the dark for sleep.
But sleep did not arrive.
So I revised my prayer
and asked instead for calm.

But what I got
was quicksand. Don't move
I thought
and you won't sink.
But I was wrong.

I sank into that heavy fluid
ground as if the night
had changed me into granite.
Eyelids stuck I tried and tried
but could not make them open.

Last night I prayed
to the sky to wake
but dawn did not arrive.
So I revised my prayer
and asked instead for calm.

MONWABISI'S SANKOFA SCARF

As facing the sea reveals the sky
and facing the sky reveals the sea
facing my soul reveals your soul
      Liu Xiaobo

In the sand a clump of fabric
I pass but can't forget   the pull
that slows me down   go back and fetch it
go ahead   Monwabisi gestures
from an ocean rock nearby
I see you   it's what we do
sunflowers on an azure weave
scarf a thriving garden he swirls
beans pumpkins mealies chives
in a dried-up township lot
sowed within our drumming hearts
from Guga S'Thebe's isi Xhosa arts
to Seapoint's highrise glitter
tourists swarming by the surf
Cape Town's gaps tear wider
like everywhere
I can't explain
feathers shatter   bones hum
Indwe blue cranes echo
songs disperse ugaba
troubles swept away
as palms together we bow
foreheads toward the ground
leaning to gather light
we follow the ones who lift us
tide and moon   it's what we do

TRAVERSING CHASMS

This other world, that world, would presumably be one
where black living matters. But we can't get there
without fully recognizing what is here.
      Claudia Rankine

Like a bird who sings above graves of stolen bones and arrowheads
then lays her eggs where silent steps still echo through her feathers

I cannot say whose music I've become traversing chasms
nothing can repeat this endless swirl of dust-filled shadows

    following

I cannot know whose dancing moves me now
my tongue has tasted how a word can spin its own return to spell

    heart

the same as earth from spiraled roots to stems unfurled
dark to light in language meant to split us we refuse

humanity distorted fear-white virus drives the news
wanting us to squeeze so tight we'd never dream this

    chorus

but we've been given open hands not separate from her wings
to hold grief's echoes sharing ground we can't imagine yet

    in joy it lives

A CROWN OF SONNETS FOR MERCY

1.

Sky blue black as indigo
sankofa bird offers her gaze
museum's backlit kkk
robe glaring frozen like a stain
of the face concealment dared
a man desperate to erase
his own mother's blood
gye nyame flags in the wind
unfurled beyond his clutch
soul-sick he turned whiter than white
lies into laws hurling flames
to line his pockets with gold
the more he buried
the deeper he stole

2.

Stolen sleep his son's soaked pillow ash-
thick cloth outspread on a cross
of pine no other spine but dread
I stand before that empty doom robe humming
wings for the dead
and still light keeps breaking
through the vast night star by star
no end to the labyrinth we shape
hands clasping near and far
stories our fearless dance creates
talons feathers beak bones
amber eyes through charred terrain
mercy's depth unknown
guides us singing through the dark woods home

3.

Dark woods leading home
I follow light on leaves and stones
in the grove's moongate we meet
as those we have lost wait at the heart
a woman from Queens has survived the klan
to be here all our steps entwined
ancient roots we have grown from
converge on the path   sun
and moon   a thousand midnight eyes
catamount wolf heron owl
no fence-wire-gash can silence
pens green as stems we swirl
on the table a blank sheet blooming
endless fields of sunflowers

4.

A sunflower spells no end in its eye
spiraled seeds and petals fly
in the face of time
we think goes on like a line
of soldiers left-right-left
no end to memory she said
how she cannot rid herself though she tries
of the trigger nor push away
countless fists aimed at her face knives
pressed hard between shoulderblades
that once were wings
how she cannot sing without feeling
sky more blue than a lifetime of blues
firebomb daggers have slashed

5.

Sun a fire not a bomb falls
as I meditate through a wood-
framed glass its curved thickness magnified
golden rays to a needle point white-
hot a boy had frozen
on an ant until a thread of smoke
rose toward his eye
crash of memory weeping pine
echo within his skull
there is no end to fury
in my hands until I dive
further into that black hole of light
distilled in a word   pupil   iris   eye
the pearl in mourning's depth is mine

6.

Every pearl leads to this
refracted moment layered moon
countless futures lost yet present
boundless voices past yet here
reverberate in the fray
of a cotton sheet human
beings forced to kneel in blood-
drenched shadows curving backward forward
spines distorted dreams unreeled
a coward's lust in the pale
of any klan-fed crowd
shrinks within like a weevil
without a field of bolls to bore
all his whitewash smeared in the rain

7.

Impossible to whitewash us
the way we dance a spell
of sunflowers humming amber light
and saltspray   hands entwined   1963
august march for freedom
death in my young-girl knees
though I couldn't walk I listened
in dreams my grandmother spun
the torn world whole as we wove
heaven's gold soaked deeper
songs like an ocean I drank
no palette of fake can separate
diamond wave from shell-flecked dune
earth from sky's unbinding blues

A SIMPLE WORD

A simple word like peace.
Two hands together, we bow.
Paz   Uxolo   Pax

Dawn breaks
yet does not shatter glass.
Joy flies out.

First the sun, then the river, finally
a swan. The moon is mute, yet softens
every jagged stone.

Clouds feather.
Petals flame.
The ground receives our pain.

Even the dead
branch blooms
a thousand shadows.

METAPHYSICS OF DOUBT

A porcupine sends sleep ahead
whenever it doubts
that peace awaits
at home in the stone
walls and ferns the river
touches to soothe.

Sleep draws the poison out
like a snake from a bottle
of alcohol. Like tea from boiled
potato peels when drunk
dissolves the gall. Rocks fall
asleep to become

a fleet of dragonflies
humming crystal wings
sounds your eyelids crave.
Such heavy lightness wakes
reflections in the river
clouds that come and go.

NOT ONE BUT THOUSANDS

Born a witness giving birth to witness
no one saw

the one my mother lost
before I breathed into view

heart within my heart
smaller than a coral rosebud

unfurling to become
waves this channeled whelk

I hold to my ear at dawn
sings for me far from the sea

though your name was never given
I've heard it

like a poem before words or an oak leaf
on a winter branch spins in time to find

every death occurs this way
the same dark revolution

songs to bear
inhabit inner faces we become

not one but thousands layered
lifting us through dusk

as music   as presence
your shadow form I harbor

BEFORE THE WORD

Layers of mist mountains hid
within   no image shimmered

from the mind of a passing glacier
that shaped the range

there below   blue as smoke
a heron clothed in silence

saw me cross the field
as I did not

see her   walking
undeterred   sky between

muted trees   marsh ice black   yellow
leaves shone through   and I

like a feather   spun
from her wing

the moment she flew
nothing left

to show we'd met
before the word invoked

first bird   then memory of
bird   everything

I know as light
not light yet

here

LIGHTNING

Lightning
pierced the stone
reflection
of my hand
its mirror
shadow glistened
as silver fish
through currents
darted to the other side
I'd never seen before
a heron swallow
a river how
she savored it
within her still
becoming as we met
ripples clouds
above below
beak to palm
we touched
as fire
entered water
and thunder
followed after
and nothing was
undone

HERON, MYSTIC, ARTIST

A tall slate blue bird walked
across the white rooftop.
Sharp talons splayed, she placed
each careful step, and turned

and paused. Feathers to shadow, stillness
liquid, every glowing curve
and the pointed beak exact,
between us steel-framed glass,

each solid pane a mirage.
I have known
before and after,
more lasting than any wound,

the feeling in her gaze
I must attempt
to dance, though I fail
again and again, such a joyous failing.

NOTES

Photographs by Janet E. Aalfs

Front Cover – *Sun Moon Shift*, Joann W. Aalfs, hooked yarn tapestry c. 1985, 2016.

Bridge Through Bamboo and Lotus, Lingyan Mountain, Suzhou, China, 2008.

Moongate at Tiger Hill/ Huqui Mountain, Suzhou, China, 2008.

Su Hui's Star Gauge, embroidered silk reproduction, Suzhou, China, 2008.

Heartstone, Colcord, West Virginia, 2012.

I. PICTURE OF THE TURNING SPHERE

p.3 *A Single Music:* Su Hui (indented lines are hers), 4th century CE, one of the earliest major Chinese poets whose work survives in the written tradition, embroidered in silk a complex 29 by 29 character spiraling grid with 5 colors. A copy hangs in the Suzhou, China silk museum where I encountered it in 2008. "Star Gauge," Hsüan-chi Tu, literally "armillary-sphere map" or "picture of the turning sphere" can be read in various directions to form roughly 3,000 smaller rhyming poems. (Reference: Hinton, David, *Classical Chinese Poetry*.) Grandmaster Yu Wen Mei: my Taiji teacher, originally from Suzhou. Xin: one word for both heart and mind.

p.12 *At Some Point:* "perspective without any point," Jane Hirshfield.

p.17 *Water Moon Guanyin:* Early 12th century wood polychrome sculpture, Boston Museum of Fine Arts.

p.18 *Channeled Whelk:* The Two-Row oniká:lha' (o knee goal)/ wampum (whelk and quahog) codified an alliance between the Haudenosaunee and the Dutch in the early 1600s...[The sacred beaded belt symbolized] two vessels traveling the river together, one for the Indian people and one for the non-native people. "We shall each travel the river together, side by side, but in our own boat. Neither of us will try to steer the other's vessel." www.oneidaindiannation.com

p.19 *Like Listening Underwater:* "Stones clapping sharp as grief" refers to a 2019 exhibit at the Rubin Museum in New York City depicting a mourning ritual for the 6th century giant Buddhas that the Taliban destroyed in 2001 in the Bamiyan Valley, Afghanistan.

p.29 *Cuneiform:* Cuneiform, the most ancient form of writing, derives from kunta, meaning female genitalia, in Sumerian of ancient Iraq... It was also spelled quna, which is the root of queen. Reference: Bertonis, Gloria M. with Carol Miranda, *Stone Age Divas: Their Mystery and Their Magic.*

p.30 *Mount Sumeru's Echo:* Mount Sumeru, at the center of the world, and of Zen enlightenment. "The iron bell struck bone," an image, called a kigo, whose meaning resists conceptualization.

p.31 *Duet:* In memory of Alin Ed Purowa, aka Princess Urduja, 14th century Phillipines, civic leader and martial arts master. The art of Kali/ Escrima/ Arnis uses rattan canes in patterns called *sinawali*, from the Tagalog word *siwali*, woven mats used as walls in nipa huts.

p.34 *Strangers:* Parts 1 & 3 contain fragments from the Dodge Poetry Festival and a college reading. Poets in the order their words appear: Anne Waldman, Victor Hernandez Cruz, Claudia Rankine, Gerald Stern, Robert Haas, Tim Siebles, Li-Young Lee, Jane Hirshfield, Khaled Mattawa.

II. 33 LOVE SONGS FOR COAL RIVER MOUNTAIN

6. Preacher: our long starving hopes, Elegy 17, John Donne; thine image stamped upon this clay, Suspiria, Henry Wadsworth Longfellow.

7. Revelations: a woman robed with sun.../ beneath her feet the moon, Revelations 12. Rule of thumb: a man was allowed to beat his wife with a rod no thicker than his thumb.

16. Montcoal: Montcoal's mining disaster, 2010. The Upper Big Branch Miners Memorial in Whitesville, WV, dedicated in July 2012, features a 48-foot black granite monument with life-size silhouettes of twenty-nine miners etched on the front.

19. Union Notes: Poetry means refusing the choice to kill or die, Adrienne Rich. Sarah Rebecca Blizzard (1864-1955) was deeply involved in union organizing. Once during the bloody 1912 miners strike in the Cabin Creek area, she was reported to have stopped a train from running by prying up the rails. She said, "That old Bull Moose would parade up and down and shoot up the woods where the miners were, so me and three other women decided one night to put an end to that. We slipped out after dark, took crowbars, pried up the rails, and rolled them down the hillside."

27. Shaft: Sub-Commissioner J. C. Symons' report, Hunshelf Bank Day Pits, England, 1842: "Girls regularly perform all the various [tasks]...just as they are performed by boys. One of the most disgusting sights I have ever seen was that of young females, dressed like boys in trousers, crawling on all fours, with belts round their waists and chains passing between their legs...the chain had worn large holes in their trousers; and any sight more disgustingly indecent or revolting can scarcely be imagined than these girls at work. No brothel can beat it." Testimony from a six year old girl in a New South Wales mine: "I have been down six weeks and make 10 to 14 rakes a day; I carry a full 56 lbs. of coal in a wooden bucket. I work with sister Jesse and mother. It is dark the time we go."

28. Strides: In honor of Violet Gathalee Pavkovich and all the women miners of Appalachia who persist.

29. Got: what's the use of all that/ noise and money… /converging gorges/ jumbled cliffs, Han-Shan #2, *Cold Mountain Poems*, Tang Dynasty, China, translation Gary Snyder. Blair Mountain continues to stand as a powerful symbol for workers of resistance, persistence, and the strength of unionization. "The [United States] has begun wrestling in recent years with its buried trauma…The Battle of Blair Mountain [1921], the culmination of a series of violent conflicts known as the Mine Wars, would also seem to be a candidate for such exhumation. The army of miners that came to Blair Mountain was made up of Black and white people, new immigrants and people with deep roots in Appalachia. They did perilous work under conditions close to indentured servitude." Reference: The New York Times, 9/6/21, Campbell Robertson.

III. WE FOLLOW WINGS

p.70 *Swallowtail at Paradise Pond:* Taoist philosopher Chang-t'zu woke up from a nap wondering, "Am I a man dreaming I'm a butterfly or a butterfly dreaming I'm a man?" This is the transformation of things. Rengetsu (1791-1875), Japanese Buddhist nun, poet, calligrapher, potter and martial artist, wrote a poem, "The Butterfly," referring to Chang-t'zu. Hokke-kyo: the name of a warbler, and the title of the Lotus Sutra.

p.72 *Giraffe's Music:* For Rose Gasherebuka who escaped Rwandan massacres during which members of her family were killed. She was inspired by the giraffes she saw as she and other women and children fled. I received the story from a mutual friend, Nobuntu Ingrid Askew.

p.73 *Anne Jeanette's Tapestry:* Anne Jeanette Aalfs Schaff, 1908-2009. Her age when she died, 101, is a palindrome.

p.77 *Folded Shadow:* Poetry's "Catbird Seat" at 60: U.S. Poets Laureate reading at the Library of Congress, 1997.

p.78 *Jonathan's Cloak:* Jonathan Holt, 1954-1994.

p.79 *Julius's Shoes:* Julius Ford, 1968-2009, racial/social justice activist, artist, educator, friend, participant in the Institute for Training and Development's 2008/2009 U.S./ South Africa performing arts teaching exchange.

p.80 *The Journey Now Requiring:* Linden Aalfs Welch, 1951-2020.

p.82 *Sonnet for the Stolen Girls:* For the g—irls kidnapped from Chibok, Nigeria, on April 14, 2014.

p.85 *Monwabisi's Sankofa Scarf:* Sankofa is a word from Ghana that means "Go back and fetch it," referring to the importance of learning where we come from. Monwabisi, d. 2017, was a gifted theater artist, gardener, and storyteller who I had the honor and pleasure to meet in Cape Town during ITD's performing arts teaching exchange in 2009.

p.87 *A Crown of Sonnets for Mercy:* The Pan-African Historical Museum U.S.A. (PAHMUSA) was founded and curated by the late LuJuana Hood, 1953-2019.

REVIEW
by
Malika Ndlovu

Reading and experiencing Janet E. Aalfs' poetry collection, *What the Dead Want Me to Know*, feels like entering a sanctuary, an old yet well tended garden in which ancient truths and current losses, haunting music and dancing shadows, all inhabit the space. Each poem is a natural 'living' sculpture of sorts. Like old trees the ground and sky have witnessed in ever-changing light over time. Like a site of remembering, where sitting with each poem spurs deeper memory and beckons you to return.

Throughout this collection, the energy of Janet's martial arts and interpretive dance practice sparkles and glints. Her poems honour the sources of these treasured teachings, and express the integration of various art forms in a method she has named *Poemotion©*. She consistently communicates reverence for the wisdom within all natural cycles. Janet's last lines often give the sense of a door opening, or a launching into flight, or a thud of falling snow, beyond conclusion.

In poems of bereavement and the profound grace of bearing witness, there is a sensory awakening that affirms the marvel of cellular memory, that no matter how much time passes, how much we change, our bodies keep detailed record. One can almost feel the chi, a following of energy, the flow of emotion that moves through and beyond the body.

In navigating grief terrain, these words, images, and story threads acknowledge human cruelties, violations, and injustices while extending empathy from the 'right here at home' zones rippling around the world. There is anchorage and extraordinary love as compass in this poet's work, a sense of 'ubuntu,' the African philosophy in which we see ourselves in each other, fully aware of our interdependence, through you am I, recognizing our common humanity and shared responsibilities.

Beyond their necessary gravity, all of these offerings invoke the vital assurance of death and dying as becoming earth, a return to elemental states, a process of surrender that we can embrace, a 'spiraling homeward.' Tapestries of bird, flight, wing, and light imagery combined with the natural shedding of skin, of body, of release from physical form, echo notions of transformation and crossing over as rebirth.

This body of work will leave deep impressions on your consciousness and feed the fire of your imagination. Allow yourself to enter its foundational stillness. Let its luminescent lines, story beams, and ancestral threads weave around and through you.

Malika Ndlovu is the author of *Truth is Both Spirit and Flesh*; *Invisible Earthquake: a woman's journal through stillbirth*; and *Close*. She is featured in *Our Words, Our Worlds: Writing on Black South African Women Poets 2000-2018*.

ABOUT THE AUTHOR

Janet E. Aalfs, 2nd poet laureate of Northampton, MA (2003-2005), 7th degree black belt and master instructor of Taiji/Qigong, Okinawan Karate, and Filipino Arnis Stick Arts, continues to share her Poemotion© weavings locally, nationally, and internationally. Founding member of Valley Women's Martial Arts, the National Women's Martial Arts Federation, and several poetry/writing groups, Janet is the founder and director of Lotus Peace Arts at Heron's Bridge/VWMA, an integrative arts non-profit community school since 1977. Dedicated to helping create sites for revelation, liberation, creative understanding, curiosity, and healing, she celebrates and enjoys life in every way she can.

Recipient of the 2013 Leadership and Advocacy in the Arts Award (CWC, UMass) and prizes for her poetry, Janet engages in peace-building through arts activism. In 2008-2009, she took part in a performing arts teaching exchange in Cape Town, South Africa, and returned there in 2018 to co-facilitate a 4-week arts intensive for young adults in one of the townships. Janet has been a Dodge Festival Poet and presenter/ performer at numerous events and conferences. She received a BA in women's studies from the University of Massachusetts/Amherst and an MFA in Poetry from Sarah Lawrence College. Her poems and essays are widely published in anthologies, journals, and online sites.

jeaalfs7@gmail.com
www.heronsbridge.org

www.ingramcontent.com/pod-product-compliance
Lightning Source LLC
Chambersburg PA
CBHW020943090426
42736CB00010B/1238